"Tip the world over on its side and everything loose will land in Los Angeles," Frank Lloyd Wright once wrote. It's true LA can feel like a wonderful collection of everything that's great about the US, while at the same time resembling absolutely no other place in the country. The city's vastness can be overwhelming at times, and sure, the traffic can be a pain, but the variety of culinary, lifestyle and outdoor activity options available makes it all worth it. After all, where else can you surf in the morning, get some work done, grab an avocado toast, go for a hike, cool down with a green juice and then celebrity-watch over dinner?

Home to a vibrant and diverse population of nearly four million people, Los Angeles is bursting at the seams with eclectic food, live music, cutting-edge art and theater, unrivaled shopping, architectural history, natural beauty and, of course, Hollywood glamour. It's impossible to sum up all that the City of Angels has to offer in a few sentences, and words often fail to do it justice – you really do have to experience it for yourself. So when you do just that, use the suggestions here to get a feel for the local flavor of this dynamic city.

the hunt

D1494385

€

Emma Specter was born and raised in New York City, went to college in Ohio and moved to Los Angeles right after graduation with a creative writing degree and without a driver's license. As it turned out, neither of those qualifications helped her find a job; after a few months of driver's ed, she found work as a writer and copyeditor, and made Los Angeles her home. When she's not covering news and entertainment for LAist.com, she can be found reading on the beach, yelling at podcasts in traffic or partaking in free samples from the Trader Joe's on Hyperion Boulevard.

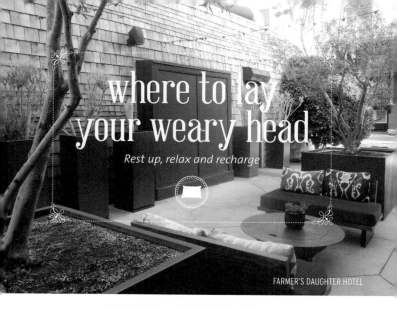

FARMER'S DAUGHTER HOTEL

FARMER'S DAUGHTER HOTEL

Perfectly situated boutique stay

115 South Fairfax Avenue (near West 1st Street; West Hollywood)
+1 323 937 3930 / farmersdaughterhotel.com
Double from $210

If you want to stay near some of LA's biggest attractions, including the Historic Farmer's Market, LACMA and The Grove, book at trendy-yet-comfy Farmer's Daughter and you'll be within walking distance of it all. The rooms adorned with hardwood floors, Adirondack chairs and plaid curtains will make you feel as if you're at a cabin retreat, albeit with some added high-end amenities (hello, rain showerhead). Make it a point to stop by Tart for a farmhouse-style brunch complete with bottomless mimosas, and don't forget to take advantage of the "jump in the pool and get 50% off your meal" deal. Some might call that embarrassing, but I call it a win-win.

HOTEL COVELL

The ultimate writer's retreat

4626 Hollywood Boulevard (near Rodney Drive; Los Feliz)
+1 323 660 4300 / hotelcovell.com
Double from $295

Hotel Covell is the definition of "storytelling in action".
Each suite represents a different chapter in the life of fictional writer George Covell, from his Oklahoma youth to his bon vivant days abroad through the rooms' eclectic furnishings and décor. The namesake's Midwest origins are referenced through rustic wood shelving and a battered prop suitcase in the Oklahoma suite, and a Rococco-style, pink velvet sofa serves as a souvenir of George's expat past in the Parisian Atelier room. This place is almost always completely booked, but if you luck out and snag a suite, you won't regret it; if not, drown your sorrows in wine by the glass at the downstairs Bar Covell.

HOTEL ERWIN

Laid-back high-rise with killer views

1697 Pacific Avenue (at 17th Avenue; Venice)
+1 310 452 1111 / hotelerwin.com
Double from $345

Long-standing Venice Beach pick Hotel Erwin has the fun, mellow vibe of an international hostel with some significant upgrades (read: you don't have to dorm with hordes of backpackers). Each room has a private balcony, a comfy pillow-top mattress, complimentary Wi-Fi, a day pass to a nearby gym and Solé bikes are available so that you can cruise along the boardwalk in style. You can also top up your stay with an in-room bubbly bar or a "bedtime story" (aka, a glass of cold milk and cookies). The Erwin's real draw, though, is its rooftop lounge; it's embarrassingly cliché to call a view "breathtaking," but I challenge anyone to look out at the city, the ocean and the mountains from the roof here and not gasp in awe.

HOTEL SHANGRI-LA

Art Deco luxury

1301 Ocean Avenue (at Arizona Avenue; Santa Monica)
+1 310 394 2791 / shangrila-hotel.com
Double from $342

If you're an architecture buff pining for the days of old California, Hotel Shangri-La was made for you. The Streamline Moderne building was inspired by the grand interiors of old-time ocean liners, so the accommodation does have a certain *Titanic* appeal (minus the sinking, of course). Fix yourself a drink from your room's minibar, pull on a flowing robe and stare out at the crashing waves of the Pacific Ocean. When you're done pretending to be Kate Winslet, head out for a hike at nearby Temescal Gateway Park (see pg 126).

HOTEL COVELL

THE CHARLIE HOTEL

Charming, storied bungalows

819 North Sweetzer Avenue (near Waring Avenue; West Hollywood)
+1 323 988 9000 / thecharliehotel.com

Double from $255

The Charlie Hotel is a rare thing: lodging that's both glam and practical.
Luminaries like Marilyn Monroe, Marlene Dietrich, Bette Davis and,
of course, Charlie Chaplin once called The Charlie home, and the
13 sumptuous cottages are each named after a famous former
inhabitant. What's more, the spaces have fully equipped kitchens
as well as washers and dryers so that you can live like an
Old Hollywood star without breaking the bank on room service.

THE CULVER HOTEL

THE CULVER HOTEL

Hollywood history comes to life

9400 Culver Boulevard (near Main Street; Culver City)
+1 310 558 9400 / culverhotel.com
Double from $279

Even if you don't reserve a room at this nearly century-old hotel
(though you should – tufted headboards, marble-topped desks and
gilded accents are de rigueur), do stop in for a drink; the building is a
National Historic Landmark and its cinematic history is unrivaled.
The Wizard of Oz cast stayed here during production and rumors persist
about the film's cast of "munchkins" using secret underground tunnels
to get from the hotel to nearby Culver Studios. Today, the Culver's
supper club mixes old-school cocktails, showcases live jazz and
screens classic films; I'll never forget sitting in the plush lobby,
sipping a Lavender Collins (vodka and crème de violette) and
watching Marlon Brando rip his shirt in *A Streetcar Named Desire*.

THE ROSE HOTEL

Beachside comforts

15 Rose Avenue (at Speedway; Venice)
+1 310 450 3474 / therosehotelvenice.com
Double from $195

The Rose Hotel is located right off Venice's raucous boardwalk,
and it can be tough to block out street noise. But what The Rose loses
in quiet, it more than makes up for in ambiance – you can wake up,
pour yourself a cup of complimentary Stumptown coffee in the sunlit
lobby, then walk exactly four minutes to the ocean. The Rose offers
the ultimate beach-bum experience with some added niceties thrown
in; the rooms are stocked with Aesop soaps, artisan chocolates and
ultrasoft bathrobes. For those kinds of amenities that close to the
water, I'll gladly take a little street noise.

highland park

Highland Park was LA's first bohemian neighborhood, and the enclave — which is young and diverse — is still the destination of choice for broke, brilliant musicians and artists drawn in by the relatively low rents and gritty-yet-relaxed energy. The northeastern locale has managed to retain its unique draw in the face of rampant gentrification (thanks to the appeal of the Craftsman- and Victorian-style homes that many have swooped in to revitalize), and most of the people you'll meet sampling Highland Park's bounty of independent coffee shops, record stores and taco trucks are Angelenos whose families have lived in the area for generations. Highland Park boasts a vibrant combination of locally owned businesses, from a typewriter repair shop to a hip-hop recording studio. It's absolutely the kind of place that should be on your radar.

1   Galco's Soda Pop Stop
2   Good Girl Dinette
3   Highland Park Bowl
4   Kitchen Mouse
5   Mount Analog
6   Pop-Hop Books & Print
7   Ramen of York
8   The Hi Hat

GALCO'S SODA POP STOP

Family-run bottle shop

5702 York Boulevard (near North Avenue 57) / **+1 323 255 7115**
sodapopstop.com / **Open daily**

It's no surprise to me that many of Highland Park's residents have been living in the area for generations. Could you leave a neighborhood that's home to an authentic soda shop that features over 700 flavors? Coming from a family of Diet Coke aficionados, I couldn't help falling in love with the emporium the first time I visited. In operation for more than a century, it was initially run as an Italian grocery store but changed directions in the 1990s when owner John – who harbored a childhood love of soda shops – began stocking carbonated drinks from small-batch, artisanal bottlers. These days, the store hawks the fizzy stuff, craft beer, cider, sake, wine, Champagne and honeymeads, as well as retro toys and vintage candy. The best kind of throwback.

GOOD GIRL DINETTE

Diner classics with a twist

110 North Avenue 56 (near North Figueroa Street)
+1 323 257 8980 / goodgirldinette.com / Closed Monday

Sometimes it's impossible to decide between pho and chicken pot pie. For those frustrating days, there's Good Girl Dinette, where you don't have to choose since the menu combines traditional Vietnamese fare and hearty American comfort food – a fusion that works unexpectedly well. Order a rice dish, like the black pepper pork confit (make sure to add the egg) and peer-pressure your meal companion to get the "Grandpa's Porridge" with mushroom and shallot; this new-meets-old menu was made for mixing and matching. Bonus: the décor is adorable, with white walls, orange counters and bright yellow seats reminiscent of the hippest elementary school you've ever seen.

HIGHLAND PARK BOWL

Boozing and bowling

5621 North Figueroa Street (near North Avenue 57)
+1 323 257 2695 / highlandparkbowl.com / Open daily

Billed as "LA's oldest bowling alley," Highland Park Bowl opened in 1927 and had a former life as punk venue Mr. T's until 1933 Group — the nightlife impresarios behind a host of refurbished bars from yesteryear — restored the space to its former glory. Today, the eight-lane bowling alley's dimly lit, wood-floored interior is chic without a hint of pretension. Highland Park Bowl's menu is a huge upgrade on your typical dive; sinking into one of the buttery-soft leather couches, sipping a Fifty Shades of Coconut (rum and matcha-infused coconut milk) and tucking into superbly cooked meatballs and calamari fritti while you wait for your turn might make you question why you've ever bowled anywhere else.

KITCHEN MOUSE

Weekend must-have

5904 North Figueroa Street (at South Avenue 59)
+1 323 259 9555 / **kitchenmousela.com** / **Open daily**

I loathe waiting for a table at trendy brunch joints, which is unfortunate since that's pretty much this town's official weekend pastime. The offerings at Kitchen Mouse, though, have lead me to make an exception to my no-queuing rule. The lines are long, but not unmanageably so, and the hearty vegan fare is worth the wait. The last Sunday morning I coaxed a group of hungry friends to make the trek here, they complained until our food came, but all was forgiven once they tasted their avocado TLTs (cherry tomatoes, avocado, lettuce and tempeh so good you forget it's healthy).

MOUNT ANALOG

All things vinyl

5906 North Figueroa Street (near South Avenue 59)
+1 323 474 6649 / climbmountanalog.com / Open daily

Mount Analog is the kind of indie record shop and concert space that's helped Highland Park build its reputation as a bona fide music haven. I bought my very first record here, shortly after buying my very first record player off Craigslist (it was a recording of Patti Smith's "Easter" that I played on a loop for six months straight). If you're a cult record label buff, take the Metro's gold line (yes, it's possible to take public transportation in LA) to the Highland stop and drop by Mount Analog to peruse records, books and clothing, or to check out one of the shop's frequent film screenings. (And, yes, the films are always related to music.)

POP-HOP BOOKS & PRINT

Word-nerd heaven

5002 York Boulevard (at North Avenue 50) / +1 323 259 2490
thepophop.com / Closed Monday

Once you've gotten your iced horchata latte at Café de Leche (see pg 20), meander next door to Pop-Hop Books & Print for the most eclectic stock of art titles, used and new fiction, zines and children's stories you'll find maybe anywhere in the city. The shop's book-lined walls will make you feel like you're hanging out in your most well-read friend's living room, and between the weighty art tomes, secondhand books and hip crafts, jewelry and greeting cards, I challenge you to make it out without buying anything.

RAMEN OF YORK

Soup for the soul

**5051 York Boulevard (near North Avenue 51) / +1 323 999 7988
ramenofyork.com / Open daily**

Round-the-block lines at Silverlake Ramen got you down? Drive 15 minutes north to their Highland Park offshoot, Ramen of York, and enjoy a bowl of their signature broth (boiled for 16 hours!) without a 16-hour-long wait. (Okay, fine, the wait at Silverlake Ramen isn't 16 hours, but I've personally waited for at least 1.5 before giving up and grabbing a slice of pizza instead.) Ramen of York's ambiance wins out, too, with a cozy counter bar and a laid-back crowd of residents washing down grilled pork belly ramen bowls with chilled glasses of amakaze (fermented rice) horchata.

THE HI HAT

Beloved live music venue

5043 York Boulevard (near North Avenue 51) / +1 323 761 0486
hihat.la / Check website for schedule

If there's a band you love that came out of LA in the last couple of years, chances are good they played The Hi Hat in their nascent days. Nestled on York Boulevard, this music venue's low-key, black-and-white façade is easy to miss – unless there's a concert raging inside. The Hi Hat used to be a pool hall, and its vibe is still down-to-earth and unpretentious despite its hipper-than-thou indie lineup made up of mostly unsigned local acts. The venue also dishes up bagels and schmear from Belle's Bagels Thursday through Sunday mornings. It's random, sure, but also wonderful.

where to caffeinate

Sit, sip and work on your screenplay

BAR NINE
3515 Helms Avenue (near National Boulevard;
Culver City), +1 310 837 7815, barnine.us, open daily

BRU COFFEEBAR
1866 North Vermont Avenue (near Franklin Avenue;
Los Feliz), +1 323 664 7500, brucoffeebar.com
open daily

CAFÉ DE LECHE
5000 York Boulevard (at North Avenue 50;
Highland Park), +1 323 551 6828, cafedeleche.net
open daily

MENOTTI'S COFFEE STOP
56 Windward Avenue (near Pacific Avenue; Venice)
+1 310 392 7232, menottis.com, open daily

STORIES BOOKS AND CAFÉ
1716 West Sunset Boulevard (near Lemoyne Street;
Echo Park), +1 213 413 3733, storiesla.com, open daily

CAFÉ DE LECHE

Los Angeles is a town of writers – or, to be more precise, unemployed writers – all seeking the same thing: the ultimate place to hole up, over-caffeinate and get to work. I've spent more hours than I care to count staring at my laptop in coffee shops around town, so I feel uniquely qualified to advise you on which ones are actually worth the $6 latte entry fee.

For the authentic struggling-Eastside-screenwriter experience, head to **Bru Coffeebar** in Los Feliz. Not only is the coffee phenomenal, it's situated on my favorite block, a stretch of Vermont Avenue that also holds Skylight Books (see pg 62), the Los Feliz Theater (see pg 86) and a host of eclectic vintage shops. The stark, well-lit space doubles as a gallery showcasing homegrown artists, as well as a meeting spot for a weekly home-brewing class called – what else? – #Homebru.

Echo Park's **Stories Books and Café** is a bookstore, coffee shop, venue and unofficial coworking space all rolled into one. Drift in anytime to browse the bookshelves, grab some fair-trade java or attend a reading on the back patio, but show up early if you want to snag a seat; the café's long tables are usually packed with aspiring scribes jotting notes in their Moleskines.

Highland Park staple **Café de Leche** roasts a mean mug of Stumptown beans, but the real draw is its ambiance – the décor, like the clientele, is modish and friendly, with free newspapers on weekend mornings, a sweet kids' area and horchata lattes for the Brooklyn-to-LA crowd.

Bar Nine is tucked away on a side street off National Boulevard, and once you've found the Culver City gem, you may never want to leave. The beans are roasted on site, and both the patrons and employees are deadly serious about their cuppas. There's no Wi-Fi, which is a mixed blessing; if you want to gulp an ultra-strong espresso and buckle down without getting distracted by Twitter, this is the place for you.

I can't recommend Venice Beach as an ideal place to write – if the ocean doesn't distract you, the boardwalk carousers will – but if you insist on trying, your best bet is **Menotti's Coffee Stop**. They pour up San Francisco fave Four Barrel Coffee (get the flat white, trust me) just two blocks from the beach. Once you've drained your cup and finished your day's work, reward yourself with a ridiculously picturesque stroll along the water.

atwater village and los feliz

Los Angeles is so vast that we Angelenos often have to shove neighborhoods together just to make sense of the city as a whole. Los Feliz and Atwater Village are a perfect example – the two areas may be separate on an official map, but they share an artsy-yet-approachable vibe that makes them cozier and somewhat more affordable than the über-trendy duo of Silver Lake and Echo Park (see pg 36). Atwater Village was put on the map by animators from the original Disney studios, while Los Feliz, one of the most diverse neighborhoods in Los Angeles, is home to Griffith Park, a large, lush urban park that features the very famous (and beautiful) Griffith Observatory. Today, Atwater Village and Los Feliz are home to some of the city's most lauded restaurants, boutiques, movie theaters, venues and galleries.

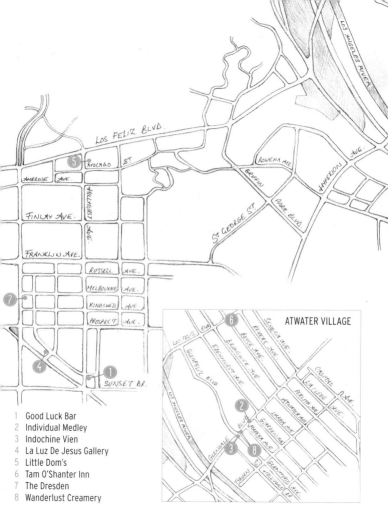

1 Good Luck Bar
2 Individual Medley
3 Indochine Vien
4 La Luz De Jesus Gallery
5 Little Dom's
6 Tam O'Shanter Inn
7 The Dresden
8 Wanderlust Creamery

GOOD LUCK BAR

Kitschy tropical drinks

1514 Hillhurst Avenue (near Hollywood Boulevard)
+1 323 666 3524 / goodluckbarla.com / Open daily

My Eastside friends and I have designated Good Luck Bar as our official first-Tinder-date place, and we're not the only ones. On packed Saturdays and chill happy-hour Thursdays alike, it's rare to pop in to the erstwhile dive and not see hordes of nervous, well-dressed people sipping Beijing Slings across from one another, their chitchat infused with a strong "do you like me?" subtext. Good Luck Bar's dim red lighting, hanging lanterns and reasonably priced (for Los Feliz, anyway) tropical cocktails make it the ideal place for dates or group hangs. Don't underestimate the Potent Potion, made of spiced rum, pineapple juice, coconut cream and nutmeg served in a (fake) hollowed-out coconut.

INDIVIDUAL MEDLEY

A boutique for the whole family

3176 Glendale Boulevard (at Garden Avenue) / +1 323 665 5344
individualmedleystore.com / Open daily

Individual Medley isn't one of those stark, snooty shops that carries just three items of absurdly expensive clothing. Though the Atwater Village store stocks finely hewn, upscale investment pieces, its inviting wood-and-leather interior and range of products for men, women and children make it a friendly space to spend time in. Individual Medley celebrates the small-town, community feel of its neighborhood, hosting a variety of events including children's book readings, "Mama Circle" morning meet-ups and even breathwork classes.

INDOCHINE VIEN

Down-to-earth Vietnamese fare

3110 Glendale Boulevard (near Madera Avenue) / **+1 323 667 9591**
indochinevien.com / **Open daily**

Nothing captures the spirit of LA quite like Vietnamese food in a strip mall, especially when we're talking mouthwatering, authentic Vietnamese food. Tucked between a Subway and an H&R Block, Indochine Vien more than delivers in flavor what it lacks in atmosphere; sit at the counter and enjoy a simple, savory meal. Pho is a perennial go-to, but I can't resist the banh xeo — mung bean and coconut crêpes filled with shrimp, chicken, tofu and onions. In fact, I once tried to replicate these in my own kitchen, an experiment that failed miserably and soon sent me back here for a taste of the real thing.

LA LUZ DE JESUS GALLERY

Surrealist Pop art

4633 Hollywood Boulevard (at Rodney Drive) / +1 323 666 7667
laluzdejesus.com / Open daily

Dedicated to showcasing LA's vibrant art scene, La Luz De Jesus was founded in 1986 by entrepreneur and Lowbrow art collector Billy Shire. The gallery describes its collections as "post-Pop with content ranging from folk to outsider to religious to sexually deviant" (so, you know, maybe don't plan a trip with your grandparents) and has launched the careers of artists including Manuel Ocampo, Robert Williams and Joe Coleman. Exhibitions are opened with a wild reception on the first Friday of each month; check it out if you're in the market for a piece or just want to mingle with the underground avant-garde.

LITTLE DOM'S

Cozy neighborhood Italian

2128 Hillhurst Avenue (near Avocado Street) / +1 323 661 0055
littledoms.com / Open daily

Think there's nothing greater than spaghetti and meatballs on a Sunday
night? I'm here to tell you there is: if you wait until Monday night, you
can take part in Little Dom's weekly three-course prix fixe supper, which
changes weekly, but always includes classic Italian comfort plates such as
corn and ricotta ravioli and buttermilk panna cotta, for under $20. It's just
like the Italian feasts my nonna used to serve up, except her menu didn't
include a $3 PBR special. (If you're not into the beer-and-red-sauce pairing,
try one of the discounted house wines.) Little Dom's is reportedly a low-key
celebrity date-night favorite, and not to name names, but I'm pretty sure I
saw Ryan Gosling at the bar once.

TAM O'SHANTER INN

Pub grub in an Old Hollywood setting

2980 Los Feliz Boulevard (near Boyce Avenue) / +1 323 664 0228
lawrysonline.com/tam-oshanter / Open daily

Come for the haggis, stay for the history. This Scottish pub and restaurant is the oldest continuously operating, same-family-owned restaurant in Los Angeles, and it boasts a Hollywood backstory worthy of its 90 years in business. John Wayne and Walt Disney were among the Inn's famous patrons back in the day. In fact, animators from the nearby Disney Studios visited the Tam O'Shanter so frequently that it was dubbed the unofficial studio commissary. Grab a seat at Walt's beloved table (#31, right by the fireplace), check out the signed Disney sketches framed on the walls and be sure to order the prime rib.

THE DRESDEN

1950s-era supper spot and cocktail lounge

1760 North Vermont Avenue (near Kingswell Avenue)
+1 323 665 4294 / thedresden.com / Open daily

Eating at The Dresden feels like you've time-traveled back to 1954...or at least landed a gig as an extra on some nostalgic TV show. The menu is staunchly retro, with nary a nod to New California cooking. When you've had all the avocado toast and green juice you can stand, it can feel like a treat to dress to the nines, sip an Old Fashioned and tuck into a shrimp cocktail or a New York strip steak. The dessert menu even boasts peach Melba – if you don't know what that is, ask your grandmother. After your meal, groove along to live jazz in the Dresden Lounge; if you're feeling musical, head over on Tuesday for open-mic night.

WANDERLUST CREAMERY

Travel-inspired ice cream

3134 Glendale Boulevard (near Madera Avenue)
+1 818 774 9888 / **wanderlustcreamery.com** / **Open daily**

LA is home to a staggering wealth of binge-worthy ice cream, but Wanderlust Creamery is in a class all its own. The flavors at this artisan shop are inspired by cities across the world, so your taste buds can globetrot without ever leaving Atwater Village. Edgy creations like the Japanese neapolitan (matcha, hojicha and black sesame) are balanced out by varieties like honey lavender, made with French lavender and California honey. There are always a host of tantalizing seasonal options, like Indonesian street crêpes (sweet cream with pandan crêpe bits and condensed milk) and the Middle East-inspired orange blossom malabi, an orange-scented cream with dates and pistachios; whatever the season, it's always fun to stop by to see what corner of the earth they're serving up.

all that blooms

Botanical fever

Los Angeles is known for its outdoor beauty, and not just on the beach. From desert cacti to bright purple jacaranda trees and hot pink bougainvillea, LA boasts a variety of flowers and plants that are just begging to be Instagrammed (or silently appreciated, if you're not the type to commit every experience to photographic memory – if so, I salute you). Although a trek through Temescal Gateway Park (see pg 126) is always lovely, you don't have to hike to see flora; you can admire the city's most beautiful petals and leaves at the spate of independent flower shops and trendy nurseries.

Potted is Atwater Village's premier destination for gorgeous, low-maintenance plants and hip garden furniture. When I moved out here, I hunted everywhere for a flawless palm to round out my first grown-up apartment, and a friendly employee helped me select a wonderfully leafy specimen that flourishes in my living room to this day.

Hearts across Silver Lake broke when **Clementine Floral Works** shuttered its Sunset Junction storefront, but luckily they relocated to nearby Burbank, where you can get their stunning arrangements delivered as an exemplary LA hostess gift, or drop in to pick up a bouquet on the go. Because what says "Thanks for having me" better than stunning blush peonies from an indie florist?

Written up in *Los Angeles Times* as "the place that's taking over your Instagram feed," Echo Park's **Cactus Store** is something of an Eastside must-see. Even if you're not in the market for a big, spiky desert plant, head over to check out the showroom, which is packed with so many rare and eclectic cacti, you'll feel like you took a trip to Death Valley without ever leaving Echo Park.

You can't talk about blossoms here without singing the praises of the **Los Angeles Flower Market**, a Downtown institution in the heart of the aptly named Flower District. Though the market closes at noon, it rewards the early riser with an array of blooms so boldly hued and plentiful, a trip there feels almost otherworldly.

Don't have a green thumb, but angling for some SoCal plant life? Succulents are the answer. **The Juicy Leaf**, a funky, eco-friendly nursery and boutique, sells succulents in handcrafted pots so stylish you'll want to hang on to them forever. They also create wonderfully weird custom terrariums, if that is your jam.

CACTUS STORE
1501 1/2 Echo Park Avenue (at Scott Avenue;
Echo Park), +1 213 947 3009, hotcactus.la
closed Monday

CLEMENTINE FLORAL WORKS
4017 Burbank Boulevard (at North Pass Avenue;
Burbank), +1 323 662 2808
clementinefloralworks.com, closed Sunday

LOS ANGELES FLOWER MARKET
754 Wall Street (near East 8th Street; Downtown)
+1 213 627 3696, originallaflowermarket.com
closed Sunday

POTTED
3158 Los Feliz Boulevard (near Glenfeliz Boulevard;
Atwater Village), +1 323 665 3801, pottedstore.com
open daily

THE JUICY LEAF
5725 North Figueroa Street (at North Avenue 58;
Highland Park), +1 310 907 5019, thejuicyleaf.com
open daily

silver lake and echo park

historic filipinotown, virgil village

Frequently referred to as the "Brooklyn of LA," Silver Lake has garnered a reputation for being one of the trendiest neighborhoods in the country, and neighboring Echo Park is just as hip. However, there's more to these enclaves than meets the eye; both may boast more than their share of ultra-stylish organic cafés, throwback speakeasies and music venues, sure, but they're also home to working families, century-old businesses and free outdoor spaces like Silver Lake Reservoir and the eponymous Echo Park. In these areas, you can buy an overpriced artisan coffee and a scrumptious $2 pupusa on the same block. I've lived in Historic Filipinotown on the outskirts of Echo Park for a year now, and nothing beats driving down Sunset at sunrise, peering up at the zigzagging array of homes and palm trees in the Silver Lake hills.

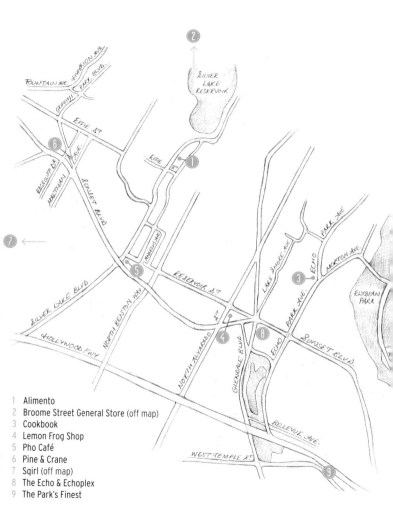

1 Alimento
2 Broome Street General Store (off map)
3 Cookbook
4 Lemon Frog Shop
5 Pho Café
6 Pine & Crane
7 Sqirl (off map)
8 The Echo & Echoplex
9 The Park's Finest

ALIMENTO

Dreamy date nights

1710 Silver Lake Boulevard (near Effie Street) / **+1 323 928 2888**
alimentola.com / **Closed Monday**

There's a reason Alimento is billed as the ultimate restaurant in Silver Lake for a romantic dinner. The sleek, cozy Italian bistro serves an inventive small-plates menu that seems designed for sharing. Careful, though: if you order something particularly delectable, like the tortellini in brodo or the octopus appetizer, it might be difficult to force yourself to let your date try a bite. Who says sharing is caring? Maybe finishing your entire meal yourself because it's so delicious is caring. And if your date is down with that, then you know they're a keeper.

BROOME STREET
GENERAL STORE

Coffee, clothes, treats and trinkets

2912 Rowena Avenue (near Herkimer Street) / +1 323 570 0405
broomestgeneral.com / Open daily

Nestled in an out-of-the-way location, Broome Street General Store is the perfect Silver Lake home base to shop, mingle or just sit outside and relax. They brew up a killer coffee from LA-based roaster Verve that is best enjoyed perched under their tree-shaded outdoor patio. Inside, they stock original, well-made clothing and accessories for men, women and children from brands like Barbour, Frame Denim and Smythe, as well as a bounteous selection of home goods that won't break the bank.

COOKBOOK

Ingredients, not recipes

1549 Echo Park Avenue (near Morton Avenue) / **+1 213 250 1900**
cookbookla.com / **Open daily**

I stumbled across Cookbook when I first moved to the Eastside, before I realized that LA wasn't exactly a walking city. I needed lemongrass for a vegetable curry I was making for a friend's birthday, and halfway through my 45-minute trudge to Vons, Cookbook — a produce haven with an emphasis on Asian vegetables — appeared in the middle of Echo Park Avenue like a mirage. Since that fateful day, I've been going back to the urban greengrocer for everything from fresh summer tomatoes and berries to locally sourced meat.

SUREK ROCK
green KALE
$3/bunch

EVITZ FARM
BLOOMSDALE SPINACH
$5

MAGGIE'S FARM
PEA SHOOTS
$5/bag

Maggie's Farm
Arugula
$5/bag

Maggie's Farm
Micro Greens
$5/bag

MA...
SA...
$

ELLWOOD FARM
COLLARDS
$3/bunch

SOUTH CENTRAL CO OP
RED CABBAGE
$3 each

GARDEN OF
FENNEL
$2.25 EA

COLORED
TRE...
#

LEMON FROG SHOP

Sartorial rainbow

1202 North Alvarado Street (near Elsinore Street) / +1 213 413 2143
lemonfrogshop.com / Open daily

Echo Park is rife with hole-in-the-wall thrift shops, but Lemon Frog Shop is truly a cut above. Stuffed to the gills with women's clothing and accessories (and the occasional unisex item), the space can feel a little overwhelming at first, but once you start digging, you'll find everything from $10 steals to wondrously preserved vintage couture. This is a great place to take in the local color, literally — it's not one of those curated, snobbish consignment stores that eschews bright hues, so vivid yellows, purples, greens and blues abound everywhere you look.

PHO CAFÉ

Herbacious Vietnamese fare

2841 Sunset Boulevard (at Silver Lake Boulevard)
+1 213 413 0888 / No website / Open daily

In my early days as a copywriter, I was taught never to use the word "hipster," as it's reductive and vague. However, I don't really know how else to describe the flannel-clad, felt-hat-wearing hordes that perennially pack under-the-radar Pho Café. The minimalist, glass-walled joint is so cool it doesn't even have a sign out front, let alone a website. To be fair, though, the crisp, flavorful menu is so good it doesn't need fanfare. If you're not into their variety of pho, explore the bun (fresh noodle) menu – the bun tom thit nuong (vermicelli rice noodles with shrimp and lemongrass steak) is always a crowd-pleaser.

PINE & CRANE

Nosh from Taiwan

1521 Griffith Park Boulevard (near Edgecliffe Drive)
+1 323 668 1128 / pineandcrane.com / Closed Tuesday

I harbor a particular affection for Pine & Crane because it happens to be the where my roommate and I signed our lease. We sat down with a plate of wonderfully puffy pork buns and instantly decided we couldn't pass up an apartment within walking distance from the most delish Taiwanese food in LA. The restaurant draws a chic, convivial crowd that spills out the door on weekend nights — for dinner, order a bottle of house rosé to complement a small-plates spread designed to be shared (don't skip the dan dan noodles, or the delectable light, flaky beef roll). If you're stopping by for an afternoon snack, though, make sure to get the house-made taro milk tea with boba.

SQIRL

Brunch for everyone

720 North Virgil Avenue, #4 (near Marathon Street)
+1 323 284 8147 / sqirlla.com / Open daily

It's hard to write anything about Sqirl that hasn't been written already in one of the restaurant's hundreds of gushing reviews. But I'll still try. The hearty-yet-healthy Virgil Village brunch mecca has practically defined the notion of New California cooking. If you, like me, are skeptical about whether the food can really live up to all the hype, take note: it can, and it always does. The sorrel pesto rice bowl with black radish and feta, accompanied by a delish Vietnamese iced coffee and a shared brioche French toast lathered with Sqirl's homemade rose geranium jam for dessert is my definition of perfection.

THE ECHO & ECHOPLEX

Live tunes galore

1822 Sunset Boulevard (near Glendale Boulevard) / +1 213 413 8200
theecho.com / Open daily

From indie rock to dance pop to death metal, there's no genre of music you won't be able to find at The Echo or its connected sister venue, Echoplex. Angelenos from all across town head here on weekends for punk shows, '90s-inspired dance parties and quirky one-off events like "Britney Spears and Justin Timberlake Night". Weeknights draw a more relaxed crowd; the free Monday night residency program spotlights hometown artists on the rise, and the rest of the week, up-and-coming indie acts like Jay Som and Frankie Cosmos take the stage.

THE PARK'S FINEST

Inventive, meat-centric eats

1267 West Temple Street (near East Edgeware Road)
+1 213 481 2800 / theparksfinest.com / Open daily

What's better than barbecue? Filipino-inspired barbecue, it turns out, especially when it's paired with an eclectic variety of craft beers from West Coast breweries like LA's own Eagle Rock Brewery. The Park's Finest features smoky, succulent cuts of tri-tip and pork alongside traditional Filipino appetizers like elote corn and bibingka (cornmeal and rice flour cornbread). Located on Temple Street in the heart of Historic Filipinotown, The Park's Finest is an ideal place for a party. The red-walled restaurant somehow always feels celebratory, even when you're just stopping in for a quick bite after work. What's more, it offers reasonably priced grub in a relaxed setting, so you can get a big group together for a fun, raucous dinner without going broke.

join the ramen craze

Way more than instant noodles

DAIKOKUYA
2208 Sawtelle Boulevard
(at West Olympic Boulevard; Sawtelle)
+1 310 575 4999, dkramen.com, open daily

SILVERLAKE RAMEN
2927 Sunset Boulevard (near North Reno Street;
Silver Lake), +1 323 660 8100, silverlakeramen.com
open daily

TATSU RAMEN
7111 Melrose Avenue (near North Detroit Street;
Hollywood), +1 323 747 1388, tatsuramen.com
open daily

TSUJITA LA
2057 Sawtelle Boulevard (at Mississippi Avenue;
Sawtelle), +1 310 231 7373, tsujita-la.com, open daily

TATSU RAMEN

The ramen craze that swept Los Angeles for years has recently given way to poke madness, but it sort of works out in your favor — while the trend followers are off chasing the latest fad, you'll have fewer round-the-block lines to deal with.

Nestled in a strip mall on Sunset Boulevard, **Silverlake Ramen** is the uber-trendy Eastside's answer to authentic Japanese ramen. Honestly? It's a pretty damn good answer. The broth here is boiled for 16 hours so that you'll be presented with a hearty, flavorful noodle bowl you'll force yourself to finish even after you're full, because it's just that tasty.

Tsujita LA is the ne plus ultra of ramen here in the City of Angels — sure, their cooked-for-60-hours tonkatsu (pork) base is delicious by itself, but the noodles are in a category all their own. They're thick, chewy, tasty: basically everything you want to twirl around a pair of chopsticks. Even in ramen-saturated Sawtelle, Tsujita is such a standout that they've recently had to open a nearby "noodle annex" to satisfy their overflow of ravenous customers.

I once went into **Daikokuya** with the worst cold of my life — raging headache, chills, sneezing, the whole nine yards — and one bowl of their fare (plus an extra egg) later, I walked out feeling completely recovered. Now, I'm not saying their salty-but-not-too-salty broth and wavy noodles have magical health-giving properties (there's a chance my Dayquil may have kicked in while I was eating), but I'm also not saying they don't.

Tatsu Ramen is an LA classic, for good reason. The larger-than-life ramen bowls are the obvious order here, with quirky names like "cheeky" (chicken broth), "hippie" (vegan broth) and, of course, "ssul" (traditional tonkatsu broth). If you're feeling adventurous, sample Tatsu's Wagyu ramen burger, which provides the ideal mixture of seasoning and crunch. Heads up: the Sawtelle branch is always packed, but the Hollywood location shines as the only broth-and-noodles fix for miles around.

chinatown

downtown, little tokyo

The borders of Chinatown, Downtown (often referred to as
"DTLA") and Little Tokyo are hard to delineate on a map,
but each of the three enclaves has its own distinct vibe and
personality. Chinatown – yes, the iconic "Forget it, Jake.
It's Chinatown." of the eponymous 1974 film –
retains architecture and history from the 1930s while
hiding a host of contemporary hidden gems; DTLA,
which is technically the business district, houses many
of the city's most exciting art and dining options; and
Little Tokyo's authentic, vibrant dining and shopping scenes
draw bustling foot traffic on a daily basis. Though very
different, these neighbors share one common factor: all
are sufficiently jam-packed with attractions to keep you
occupied all day and into the night. Oh, actually, they share
two common factors: they also all have notoriously terrible
parking options. Luckily, they're all subway-navigable,
if you're up for a trip on the newly improved Metro.

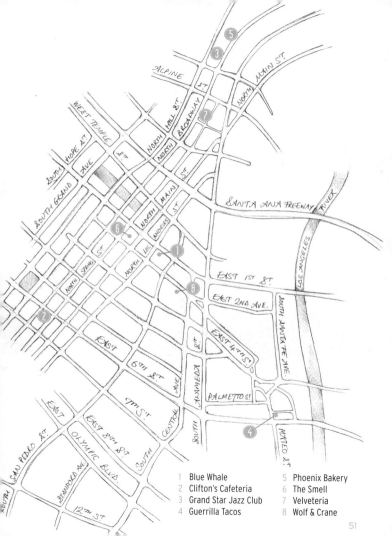

1 Blue Whale
2 Clifton's Cafeteria
3 Grand Star Jazz Club
4 Guerrilla Tacos
5 Phoenix Bakery
6 The Smell
7 Velveteria
8 Wolf & Crane

51

BLUE WHALE

Live jazz in Little Tokyo

Weller Court Plaza, 123 Astronaut E S Onizuka Street, Suite 301 (near East 1st Street) / +1 213 620 0908 / bluewhalemusic.com Open daily, closed the first Sunday of every month

If you're just dying to live out your *La La Land* fantasy by listening to a jazz trio in a dark, hazy hole-in-the-wall, Blue Whale is the place to do it. This bar and jazz club has been catering to music lovers since 2009, featuring a mixture of new and established acts and a revolving series of art exhibits to boot. If the music doesn't sway you, odds are the cocktail list will. Try the bourbon chai (chai-infused bourbon, coffee, maple syrup and cream) for a sweet shock to the system. The joint also serves a curated small-plates menu — my picks are the shrimp tempura tacos and the cheese plate, which features a variety of aged French and Californian cheese — perfect to nibble at while you close your eyes, sip your drink and listen.

CLIFTON'S CAFETERIA

Swing dancing, taxidermy and drinks

648 South Broadway (near 7th Street) / +1 213 627 1673
cliftonsla.com / Closed Monday

As its name would suggest, Clifton's Cafeteria does serve food, but I've never actually taken the time to eat there – it's too hard to resist the dance floor. The joint opened in 1935 and abounds with bizarre décor: there's a stuffed grizzly in one room, and a life-size faux Redwood dominates the center of the space. The retro vibe is no less quirky, with a dedicated swing dancing floor across from a more traditional DJ area that sometimes finds itself hosting the occasional impromptu burlesque show in addition to big bands on Friday and Saturday nights. When you need a break from rock stepping, wander around to explore all the architectural secrets Clifton's has to offer – and don't miss the tiki bar on the top floor.

GRAND STAR
JAZZ CLUB

Throwback space, modern pace

Chinatown Central Plaza
943 Sun Mun Way (near Lei Min Way)
+1 213 626 2285
grandstarjazzclub.com
Closed Monday and Tuesday

This town is rife with reimagined dance
halls and genuinely gritty dive bars – but
usually those two concepts don't go hand in
hand. At Chinatown's Grand Star Jazz Club
though, they do. The venue puts on fun,
high-energy themed events, like French Pop
Night, and brings in diverse bands ranging
from hip-hop to DJ sets to, of course, jazz.
It's completely acceptable to either dance
the night away or order yourself a beer
and glower in the corner. Opened in 1946,
this joint serves Vietnamese fare until 7pm
nightly; but when you head out of the
nightclub at 2am, desperate for sustenance
after singing along to Serge Gainsbourg
all night, you'll have your pick of 24-hour
restaurants within stumbling distance.

GUERRILLA TACOS

Traditional-meets-new street tacos

582 Mateo Street (at Willow Street)
No phone / guerrillatacos.com
Closed Tuesday

Trying to find the premier taco truck in LA is like trying to find the best bagel in NYC — there's such an overwhelming number of amazing candidates that the sampling process is a joy in itself. Parked in Downtown on Mondays, Guerilla Tacos is a top contender — the bold, inventive menu includes an array of options like the roasted sweet potato taco with almond chile, fried corn nuts, scallions and feta, and a particularly toothsome ahi tuna tostada. After one taste, it's easy to see why fancy food mags swoon over chef Wes Avila's tacos — for the price of street food, you're walking away with a world-class meal. Can't make it on Monday? Check the website for the other locations throughout the week.

PHOENIX BAKERY

Dim sum and confections

969 North Broadway (at Bamboo Lane) / **+1 213 628 4642**
phoenixbakeryinc.com / Open daily

The Chinatown here may not be as big as San Francisco's or New York's,
but it more than holds its own in the cuisine category. Local institution
Phoenix Bakery is a big part of the reason why. Opened in 1938 by the
same family that still operates it today, Phoenix dishes up cheap, delectable
treats like steamed pork buns, almond cookies and "sticky sugar butterflies"
(deep-fried wonton skins drenched in syrup). The real standout, though, is
its booming birthday cake business. Nothing says "I love you so much I drove
to Chinatown in rush-hour traffic" like Phoenix's signature strawberry cake,
which is ornately decorated with icing and sugar flowers.

THE SMELL

Alternative music and art space

247 South Main Street (near Harlem Place) / **No phone**
thesmell.org / **Check website for schedule**

The Smell is one of the last surviving bastions of LA's underground punk scene. Opened in 1998 as a DIY, community-oriented arts and performance venue, the all-ages, booze-free club has featured a host of up-and-coming California rockers, including Ty Segall and No Age. The volunteer-run venue is accessible to all, with most shows costing just $5. It's an ongoing challenge to keep a not-for-profit brick and mortar open for business as rents in the neighborhood skyrocket, so head down to DTLA to see some real rock while you still have the chance.

VELVETERIA

Velvet paintings galore

711 New High Street (near Ord Street) / **+1 503 309 9299**
velveteria.com / **Closed Tuesday**

The Velveteria Epicenter of Art Fighting Cultural Deprivation (or simply,
Velveteria) is owned by Caren Anderson and Carl Baldwin, whose vast
personal collection of velvet paintings eventually grew so large that they
opened a museum. For a nominal fee, you can stop by and see 450 of their
3,000-strong, wonderfully kitsch collection for yourself. There are velvet
portraits of luminaries from California governor Jerry Brown to Clint Eastwood
to Snoop Dogg. And, of course, plenty of the requisite horse paintings.

WOLF & CRANE

For whiskey lovers and beer swillers alike

366 East 2nd Street (near South Central Avenue)
+1 213 935 8249 / **wolfandcranebar.com** / **Open daily**

Wolf & Crane is the kind of cozy-looking, convivial bar you pass on the way home from work that suddenly makes you think "Huh, I could go for a beer". A pint is the unofficial drink of choice at this hip, no-frills watering hole, but the drink menu also boasts a wide array of Taiwanese whiskeys, as well as an impressive cocktail list (how could any '90s music fan pass up a drink called the "Fiona Apple"?). Wolf & Crane goes above and beyond most neighborhood bars in customer satisfaction: you can place a delivery order for an artisan pizza from nearby Pitfire Pizza right at the bar on weekdays.

literary outposts

Get lost in the stacks

Los Angeles is stereotyped as being less than literary, but the city is more book-friendly than it seems. Hometown authors like Maggie Nelson and Paul Beatty have helped define the modern LA experience, and we tout literary events from the *Los Angeles Times* Festival of Books to the Printed Matter's LA Art Book Fair. Then, there are our killer bookstores. If you're a bibliophile of any stripe, you'll be very happy in any of these.

Skylight Books is every visiting author's first stop for book signings, for good reason. The award-winning shop is situated on one of the coolest blocks in Los Feliz, but the vibe is down-to-earth enough that you can spend hours browsing the aisles without anyone bothering you.

If you've got an hour (or two) to kill in Hollywood, **Counterpoint Records and Books** is the place to go; the shelves of insanely well-priced used fiction are countered only by their crates full of vintage vinyl. I scored a copy of Zadie Smith's *On Beauty* here for a measly $4 while waiting around for a show to start at the UCB Theater nextdoor.

Even if you're not particularly into book shopping, **The Last Bookstore** is a must. The multistory space features a tunnel made entirely out of books, a host of artists' galleries and an incredible selection of rare and foreign volumes. Craving local reads? The carefully curated "Los Angeles Lit" section will set you up with all the Joan Didion and John Fante you need to truly understand this town.

Book Soup isn't your typical used-book joint. The upscale West Hollywood shop has, in its own words, "been serving readers, writers, artists, rock 'n' rollers, and celebrities since 1975". If you're looking for the ultimate written history of

Hollywood, Book Soup is your place — and make sure to stock up on the shop's book-and-movie-title matchboxes, which make for perfect souvenirs.

I have a little ritual I perform whenever I'm in Sawtelle: I put my name down at Tatsu Ramen (see pg 48), and during the hour-plus wait for a table, I make the 10-minute walk over to **SideShow Rare & Remarkable Books, Art & Curiosities**. This Westside purveyor showcases rare comic books alongside the collected works of Kant to great effect. It can be hard to pull yourself out of here, which is why I ensure I have the promise of ramen hanging over my head whenever I walk in.

BOOK SOUP
8818 Sunset Boulevard (near Horn Avenue;
West Hollywood), +1 310 659 3110, booksoup.com
open daily

COUNTERPOINT RECORDS AND BOOKS
5911 Franklin Avenue (near North Bronson
Avenue; Hollywood), +1 323 957 7965
counterpointrecordsandbooks.com, open daily

SIDESHOW RARE & REMARKABLE BOOKS,
ART & CURIOSITIES
11323 Idaho Avenue (near Corinth Avenue; Sawtelle)
+1 310 428 4631, sideshowbookstore.com, open daily

SKYLIGHT BOOKS
1818 North Vermont Avenue (near Russell Avenue;
Los Feliz), +1 323 660 1175, skylightbooks.com
open daily

THE LAST BOOKSTORE
453 South Spring Street (near West 5th Street;
Downtown), +1 213 488 0599, lastbookstorela.com
open daily

THE LAST BOOKSTORE

koreatown

mid-wilshire, miracle mile

You can drive from Koreatown to Mid-Wilshire in a few minutes, but doing all the cool stuff these neighborhoods have to offer will take significantly longer. Koreatown is known for its amazing food, spas and lively bar scene (seriously, don't miss your chance to belt out '80s hits at any of the karaoke spots), and in Mid-Wilshire and Miracle Mile, you can cross off bucket-list venues like LACMA and the La Brea Tar Pits, then head to Little Ethiopia for some seriously delish food. Parts of these areas tend to be quieter and more residential, which makes them well-suited for family visits – plus, they're centrally located, so you're basically equidistant from the shores of Venice Beach and the bars of the trendy Eastside.

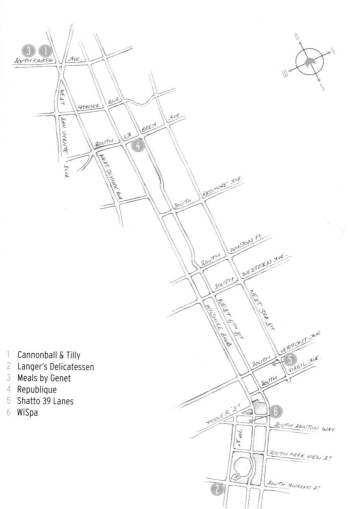

1 Cannonball & Tilly
2 Langer's Delicatessen
3 Meals by Genet
4 Republique
5 Shatto 39 Lanes
6 WiSpa

CANNONBALL & TILLY

Curated mix of eclectic, pre-loved goods

1029 South Fairfax Avenue (near West Olympic Boulevard)
+1 323 384 2640 / cannonballandtilly.com / **Open daily**

This town's abundance of vintage shops can normally be divided into two categories – the hyper-expensive designer boutiques and the overcrowded, cheap thrift shops. Cannonball & Tilly is a colorful, chaotic fusion. Step inside the Mid-Wilshire shop and you're likely to find a mint-condition Gucci scarf hanging next to a frayed baby-doll dress that costs $5. This emporium boasts a particularly well-stocked accessories section, with real amethyst and lapis sparkling behind the counter. Half the fun here is hunting for treasure at a variety of price points, and you're practically guaranteed to leave with at least one sartorial souvenir.

LANGER'S DELICATESSEN

The best pastrami maybe anywhere

704 South Alvarado Street (at 7th Street) / +1 213 483 8050
langersdeli.com / Closed Sunday

I grew up in New York City, so it feels like utter blasphemy to declare any pastrami outside the five boroughs the tastiest in the country. That said, the pastrami at Langer's Delicatessen is so incredible it could coax even the most die-hard of New Yorkers out to the Golden Coast. The old-school Jewish deli has been doling out comfort food since 1947, and the menu remains blessedly unchanged, down to the cheese blitzes and noodle kugel. Fair warning: Langer's closes at 4pm, so make sure to work in a trip for lunch...or for breakfast, if you don't mind starting your day with a heaping plate of spicy, smoked meat.

MEALS BY GENET

Stand-out Ethiopian feast

1053 South Fairfax Avenue (near Whitworth Drive) / **+1 323 938 9304**
mealsbygenetla.com / **Closed Monday and Tuesday**

As you might expect, the Little Ethiopia strip of Mid-Wilshire overflows with amazing, authentic East African eats. The can't-miss destination of the neighborhood, though, is Meals by Genet. Make a reservation and get a (big) group together to enjoy chef Genet Agonafer's fragrant, family-style platters, which include an array of flatbread, spices and your choice of beef, lamb, chicken or delectable veggies. Don't leave without sampling the traditional, tangy injera bread (it even comes in gluten-free form made with teff), and most of all, come hungry, because this is not the place to pick at a salad.

624 South La Brea Avenue (near West 6th Street) / +1 310 362 6115
republiquela.com / **Open daily**

If you're looking to treat yourself to a fancy, outstanding meal, Republique is the place. Sure, the red wine-braised beef short rib will set you back a bit and the price point of the steak frites might give you sticker shock, but the dishes here are worth the money. My picks? The Maine lobster spaghetti and the grilled octopus salad. What's more, you'll be savoring your gourmet dinner in a historic building built by Charlie Chaplin in 1928, and the in-house bakery serves a dizzying array of flaky pastries and Paris-quality baguettes that won't break the bank.

SHATTO 39 LANES

Bowling and arcade games, grown-up style

**3255 West 4th Street (at South Vermont Avenue) / +1 213 385 9475
shatto39lanes.com / Open daily**

Who says bowling is for kids? Koreatown's dimly-lit, divey Shatto 39 Lanes is the ultimate venue for a low-key outing. It's the kind of sticky-floored, beer-serving bowling alley you hung out at in college, not one of those painfully hip reimagined experiences that charges an arm and a leg for a pair of rented shoes. Opened in 1954, this spot even has a clutch selection of arcade games, so you can relive your misspent youth playing Ms. Pac-Man (or billiards, if you're classy). Then there's the $4 cocktails, which make for an automatic good time. Beware, though: the drinks are strong and sugary, so do remember to hydrate and save yourself from a nasty hangover.

WISPA

Get your spa on

2700 Wilshire Boulevard (at South Rampart Boulevard)
+1 213 487 2700 / wispausa.com / Open daily

I never thought hot tubs and clay saunas would go with Korean soap operas and massive amounts of bibimbap, but WiSpa is proof that the combination works. Located in vast Koreatown, WiSpa boasts the leading 24-hour K-spa experience this side of Seoul. Korean grandmas and Eastside hipsters alike fill the steamy saunas for the $25 entry fee. If you're visiting with a group, split up for sex-segregated hot-tub soaks and cold-water plunges, then reunite over Korean barbecue in the co-ed area. (Or not... my friend once brought a bad date here, then spent the entire night in the women's sauna avoiding him.) If you want to add on a massage or facial to the experience, those are available for a little bit extra.

hollywood

beverly hills, sherman oaks, west hollywood

Most people know Beverly Hills, Hollywood and West Hollywood ("WeHo," to locals) as three of LA's fanciest, schmanciest neighborhoods. And they're not entirely wrong – there are plenty of upscale art museums, chichi boutiques and fine-dining restaurants between the enclaves, but these hoods are also chock-full of marvelous yet unassuming venues. Hollywood is a treasure trove of offbeat galleries and record stores, and WeHo offers more than its share of cutting-edge movie theaters and vintage clothing haunts. Beverly Hills can be a little harder to enjoy if your budget isn't unlimited, but it does offer a wealth of amazing architecture; check out the storybook-style "Witch's House" on Walden Drive or the mid-century modernist Stahl House in the Hills, for starters.

The suburb of Sherman Oaks may be largely residential and family-friendly, but that doesn't necessarily mean it's boring. Drop by for an hour or two, if for no other reason than to say you've been to the Valley.

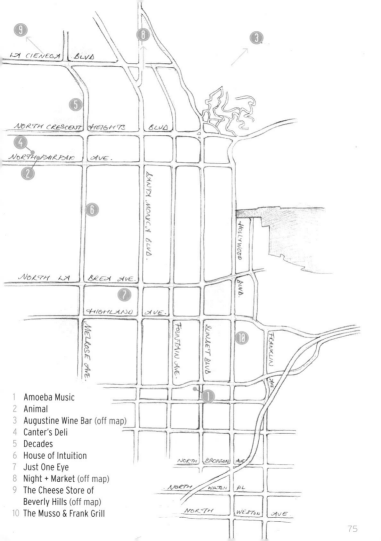

1 Amoeba Music
2 Animal
3 Augustine Wine Bar (off map)
4 Canter's Deli
5 Decades
6 House of Intuition
7 Just One Eye
8 Night + Market (off map)
9 The Cheese Store of
   Beverly Hills (off map)
10 The Musso & Frank Grill

AMOEBA MUSIC

Seminal record store

6400 Sunset Boulevard (near Ivar Avenue) / **+1 323 245 6400**
amoeba.com / **Open daily**

Amoeba Music has been the epicenter of LA's indie music scene for years.
Opened in 2001, the Hollywood music haunt has persisted even as record
stores have become increasingly anachronistic; Amoeba still boasts the
biggest selection of vinyl, CDs, DVDs and merch in town. What's more,
this is a must-visit when indie artists are in the city. It's not uncommon
for Angelenos to stop by to grab a new LP and be treated to live sets from
musicians such as Sylvan Esso and Ryan Adams.

ANIMAL

Big on meat, small on plates

435 North Fairfax Avenue (near Rosewood Avenue) / **+1 323 782 9225**
animalrestaurant.com / **Open daily**

Vegans beware: meat constitutes the glowing centerpiece of virtually
every meal at Animal (perhaps unsurprisingly, given the name). Foods you
never knew were edible – think chicken liver, fried rabbit legs, pig ear and
offal – are served up with gusto at this institution of fine dining from famed
restaurateurs Jon Shook and Vinny Dotolo. The real surprise? Everything is
absolutely delicious. If the meat-centric dinner menu is just too bloody for
you, Animal also serves up a killer brunch that's full of vegetarian-friendly
options like hemp granola and cornmeal waffles.

AUGUSTINE WINE BAR

In vino veritas

13456 Ventura Boulevard (near Sunnyslope Avenue)
+1 818 990 0938 / augustinewinebar.com / Open daily

This tiny, charming enoteca is a gem of the Valley, perfect for a romantic date, grabbing a quick drink with a friend or impressing your wine-loving family members when they're in town. The space is both hip and sophisticated with its exposed timber beams, concrete floor and velvet-upholstered booths; classic yet current with a vibe that's upscale but not pretentious. As for the wine, they've got a huge collection of vintage vintages, but are just as happy to pour you a more reasonably priced glass — and even happier when helping you select the superlative sip. Bonus tip: don't miss their snacks. The sunchoke toast appetizer will rock your world.

CANTER'S DELI

24-hour Jewish delicatessen

419 North Fairfax Avenue (near Oakwood Avenue) / +1 323 651 2030
cantersdeli.com / Open daily

Canter's stands apart from all the Jewish eateries in all of Los Angeles.
Sure, Langer's (see pg 69) serves killer pastrami, and Nate 'n Al of Beverly
Hills toasts a mean bagel, but ask anyone who knows their delis and they'll
tell you Canter's is the real thing. In operation since 1931, there's something
about the atmosphere — down-to-earth, authentic, slightly dingy, open at all
hours — that makes everything served here, from matzo brei to the Little New
Yorker fish sandwich, taste amazing. Next time you find yourself on Fairfax in
the wee small hours, do yourself a favor: go into Canter's and order a slice of
chocolate babka. By the time the last bite is gone, you'll find yourself ready to
take on the world.

DECADES

Upscale resale

8214 Melrose Avenue (near North Harper Avenue) / +1 323 655 1960
decadesinc.com / Open daily

West Hollywood has developed a reputation as a consignment shopper's paradise, with high-flying fashion mavens flocking to the neighborhood to sell their season-old goods. If you want to try your hand at scoring something sartorially luxe, make a stop at Decades. The shop mixes pre-loved high-design items with a wide range of vintage couture, offering one-of-a-kind Chanel and Gaultier pieces alongside edgy contemporary labels like Balmain and Vivienne Westwood. Even if the price tags are too steep for you, it's worth paying a visit to the Melrose shop, which feels like taking a brightly hued tour through fashion history.

HOUSE OF INTUITION

Catering to your metaphysical needs

7449 Melrose Avenue (at North Vista Street) / **+1 213 413 8300**
houseofintuitionla.com / **Open daily**

Your trip to La La Land won't be complete until you've partaken in every SoCal stereotype, including a visit to spiritual supply store, House of Intuition. Though this emporium has expanded to the Eastside lately, the original WeHo locale is the go-to for all things spiritual. Don't be surprised if you run into faces you know from the tabloids in the well-stocked "crystals," "incense" and "tarot" sections. Whether you truly believe in supernatural healing and the power of prayer candles or just want to stock up on bath bombs and rose water, House of Intuition has what you're looking for.

JUST ONE EYE

Eclectic boutique and art space

7000 Romaine Street (near North Orange Drive) / **+1 888 563 6858**
justoneeye.com / Closed Sunday

Once the former digs of reclusive tycoon Howard Hughes, the Art Deco-style building Just One Eye occupies has heaps of bona fide Hollywood history. These days, the store is packed to the brim with edgy designer goods from makers like Yohji Yamamoto and Costume National. Even if you're not looking to buy, the art is worth a trip all on its own, with pieces from contemporary luminaries like Damien Hirst displayed on the walls. The frequent events with haute brands like Cartier and Christopher Kane are trés chichi, but worth checking out — particularly if you're hoping to catch a glimpse of the LA fashion and art world in party mode.

NIGHT + MARKET

Rebellious Thai food

9043 Sunset Boulevard (near North Wetherly Drive)
+1 310 275 9724 / nightmarketsong.com / **Closed Sunday**

Los Angeles is home to some of the tastiest Thai cuisine in America, and chef Kris Yenbamroong has played a big part in helping create that reputation. His colorful eatery, Night + Market, consistently lands on every major "best of" list, for good reason — the small plates overflow with bright flavor. The khao soi gai, a sweet-and-spicy curried noodle dish, is so toothsome it will have you scraping your bowl for more, and the vibrant, eclectic plating of traditional recipes like larb and papaya salad make a meal here a treat for all the senses.

THE CHEESE STORE OF BEVERLY HILLS

Gourmet grocer

419 North Beverly Drive (near Brighton Way) / **+1 310 278 2855**
cheesestorebh.com / **Open daily**

Calling all charcuterie obsessives: don't skip a trip to The Cheese Store of Beverly Hills, where a dedicated staff has been advising visitors on artisanal pairings of wine, cured meats, bread and, of course, fromage since 1967. More than a shop hawking high-end picnic accoutrement, The Cheese Store offers a rotating series of events, including a "Master Grilled Cheese Class" (who among us could not benefit from learning how to make a gourmet-quality grilled cheese sandwich?). RSVPs are required for the shop's monthly tasting events, so be on the lookout for registration; otherwise you'll miss out on tempting offerings like "The Wines & Cheeses of The Loire Valley".

THE MUSSO & FRANK GRILL

Martinis-and-steak splurge

6667 Hollywood Boulevard (near North Cherokee Avenue)
+1 323 467 7788 / mussoandfrank.com / Closed Monday

There's nowhere quite like The Musso & Frank Grill. Frequently billed as the oldest restaurant in Hollywood, this joint opened in 1919 and has been slinging cocktails and oysters ever since. The steakhouse gained notoriety in the 1930s as a hangout for disgruntled novelists-turned-screenwriters, and the menu remains largely unchanged since the days when F. Scott Fitzgerald, William Faulkner and Raymond Chandler stopped in for mint juleps and cuts of prime rib. Though Hollywood Boulevard has changed a lot since then, with souvenir shops and strip clubs cropping up on every corner, you can still slide into a leather booth here for a taste of Old Hollywood glamour.

silver screens

LA's foremost independent cinemas

LOS FELIZ THEATER
1822 North Vermont Avenue (at Russell Avenue; Los Feliz), +1 323 664 2169
vintagecinemas.com/losfeliz, open daily

NEW BEVERLY CINEMA
7165 Beverly Boulevard (near North Formosa Avenue; West Hollywood), +1 323 938 4038
thenewbev.com, open daily

SILENT MOVIE THEATRE
611 North Fairfax Avenue (near Clinton Street; Hollywood), +1 323 330 4412, cinefamily.org
open daily

THE EGYPTIAN THEATRE
6712 Hollywood Boulevard (near North Las Palmas Avenue; Hollywood), +1 323 461 2020
egyptiantheatre.com, open daily

VISTA THEATRE
4473 Sunset Drive (near Sunset Boulevard; Los Feliz) +1 323 660 6639, vintagecinemas.com/vista
open daily

THE EGYPTIAN THEATRE

The entertainment industry has been a staple of LA's economy since the Roaring Twenties, and these days, nowhere is more associated with movie magic than Hollywood. While the business of filmmaking has changed a good amount, plenty of the old-school movie houses are still open for business – visit any of these classic theaters to get a taste of authentic moviegoing.

Though it's a Hollywood landmark you might think you should avoid, **The Egyptian Theatre** is now the permanent home to American Cinematheque, which screens classics like Bram Stoker's *Dracula* alongside contemporary indie films. Opened in 1922 and built by Sid Grauman, it's worth fighting the crowds of impersonators and selfie-takers to get inside here and behold the lovingly restored, gilded interior.

Quentin Tarantino fans will get a major kick out of the **New Beverly Cinema**, an arthouse cinema in a West Hollywood building dating back to the 1920s that is owned and curated by the auteur himself. The New Beverly screens 35mm film prints of artsy work and cult double features, as well as Tarantino movies during packed midnight showings on Fridays. Want to stop by for something more family-friendly? There's a Saturday morning matinee series just for you.

The vintage **Los Feliz Theater** is a fab spot for a movie date. Built in 1923, the kitschy neon façade is unmissable, and the ticket prices are unbeatable – most shows are $10, which is less than most cinemas in town, so you can apply the savings to popcorn and candy. Then there's Los Feliz's single-screen **Vista Theatre**. It was originally a vaudeville venue when it opened in the '20s; now, the landmark shows new releases while retaining its historic architecture.

West Hollywood's historic **Silent Movie Theatre** is now run by Cinefamily, a non-profit dedicated to bringing LA's cinephile community together over the likes of David Lynch's oeuvre. Other than projecting modern indie films, the theater hosts the beloved Movie Interruption series, wherein comedians share their thoughts about a film like *Mean Girls* during the screening, "Animation Breakdown" (Saturday morning cartoons) and "Hangover Matinees" on Sunday afternoons.

culver city and west adams

The Westside neighborhood of Culver City has a rich history of Hollywood lore and speakeasy allure; the sprawling MGM Studios were originally headquartered here (on what's now the Sony Studios lot), and during the Prohibition Era, landmarks like The Culver Hotel (see pg 9) doubled as illicit hooch joints. West Adams is a more youthful, residential part of LA, boasting one of the largest collections of historic houses on the West Coast – take a walk and you're likely to come across Arts and Crafts, Beaux Arts, Colonial Revival and Craftsman-style homes, among a host of many others. Today, Culver City and West Adams offer a wide array of bars, restaurants, shops and nightlife activities, with more options being added seemingly by the minute. I used to live in between the two areas, and I marveled at the cool new locales that were constantly cropping up without eroding the historic character.

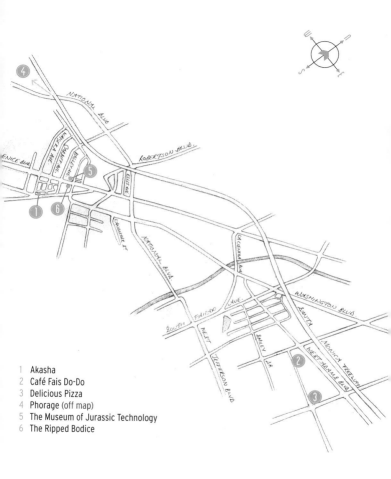

1 Akasha
2 Café Fais Do-Do
3 Delicious Pizza
4 Phorage (off map)
5 The Museum of Jurassic Technology
6 The Ripped Bodice

AKASHA

Farm-to-table New American dishes

9543 Culver Boulevard (at Watseka Avenue) / **+1 310 845 1700**
akasharestaurant.com / **Open daily**

Located in the historic Hull Building, Akasha serves a seasonal, locally influenced small-plates menu that diners can't stop talking about (if the short ribs and sweet potato ginger purée are available when you swing by, order them). The customer base here is built primarily of the power-lunch crowd due to its proximity to the Sony Studios headquarters, which makes it a particularly good place for some good, old-fashioned eavesdropping. After all, what could be a purer LA experience than overhearing studio gossip while sipping a cup of house-roasted Intelligentsia coffee?

CAFÉ FAIS DO-DO

Down-to-earth live concert hall

5257 West Adams Boulevard (near South Cloverdale Boulevard)
+1 323 931 4636 / faisdodo.com / Check website for schedule

This divey, fun music venue's name is taken from the French expression "fais do-do," which means "go to sleep" — stop into one of the monthly burlesque performances, and you'll see that the name is perhaps a tad ironic. Café Fais Do-Do's patrons often stay until the wee hours at a diverse assortment of events, including live shows that range from rap to reggae to Latin rock to jazz to R&B and beyond, so there's something to satisfy everyone. Architecture buffs will plotz at the Art Deco features — there's even a romantic balcony that overlooks the vibrant scene.

DELICIOUS PIZZA

Hip-hop pizza shop

5419 West Adams Boulevard (near South Burnside Avenue)
+1 323 424 3014 / **deliciouspizza.com** / **Open daily**

Delicious Pizza caters to music fans and foodies alike. The joint's gourmet-quality pies made with an organic grain mix and natural yeast starter will please even the fussiest pizza aficionados. I love the Cheeba Cheeba with its mushrooms, soppressata and shallots, but the Yacht Club will delight if you, like me, are pro-anchovy. If you're around on the second Sunday of a month, check out the Rum Punch Brunch; it boasts the Belly Bomb Breakfast, which consists of ricotta pancakes, two eggs, hash browns, ciabatta and bacon, and is not for the faint of heart. More than just nosh, the shop's kick-ass collection of hip-hop memorabilia is sure to wow.

PHORAGE

Flavorful, sustainable Vietnamese

3300 Overland Avenue (at Rose Avenue) / +1 310 876 0910
phoragela.com / Open daily

If you want to enjoy a truly great Asian meal in Los Angeles, you may just have to get comfortable eating in casual surroundings. Much like Silverlake Ramen (see pg 48) and Indochine Vien (see pg 26), Phorage is nestled in a strip mall, but the pho eatery's simple exterior hides a tasty, locally sourced menu that's hip without crossing over into hipster territory. The fresh, organic produce Phorage uses in its meals — particularly the moreish veggie roll packed with mushrooms, cabbage, mint and vermicelli, and tangy green papaya salad with crispy tofu, shrimp, shallots, roasted peanuts and a fish sauce vinaigrette — will leave you feeling light, rather than bloated. Plus, their hangover tonic that's less than $3 is sure to put some pep in your step.

THE MUSEUM OF JURASSIC TECHNOLOGY

Eclectic exhibits and a rooftop garden

**9341 Venice Boulevard (near Bagley Avenue) / +1 310 836 6131
mjt.org / Open Thursday through Sunday**

You can keep your MoCAs and your LACMAs; nestled in Culver City, The Museum of Jurassic Technology is one of LA's incomparable hidden gems. Dedicated to "public appreciation of the Lower Jurassic period," the museum curates natural history and science exhibits that are fun for kids and adults alike. For example, they recently put on the wonderfully esoteric *Garden of Eden on Wheels: Collections from Los Angeles Area Mobile Home Parks*, which is definitely something you won't find at The Getty. The tiny, intriguing museum's rooftop café is a marvelous place to sip a latte and ruminate on the mysteries of life.

THE RIPPED BODICE

Romance junkies, rejoice

3806 Main Street (near Venice Boulevard) / +1 424 603 4776
therippedbodicela.com / Closed Monday

Opened in 2016 by sisters Bea and Leah Koch, The Ripped Bodice is the first bookstore in the US of A to exclusively stock romance novels. The emporium is wholly devoted to the art of devouring guilty pleasures: the place is packed with all the steamy beach reads you'll ever need, and the shelves are classified by genre, ranging from historical fiction to erotica to more niche options, like time travel, cowboys and even a slew of books set during Christmas. In addition to literature, there's also a treasure trove of apparel with T-shirts that proclaim "Smart Girls Read Romance" and massive, store-branded totes. The purveyor also hosts a wide range of community events and programs for authors and readers, so definitey check the website to see what's happening when you're in town.

flea market fix

The definitive guide to scoring the coolest finds

Flea market shopping in LA is a lot like dating in LA; you have to be organized, methodical and very resilient. If you avoid the crappy street fairs that try to sell you a batik tank top for $80, you can find all sorts of goodies, from Old Hollywood-era evening gowns to framed vintage movie posters.

Silver Lake Flea is the trinket collector's best friend. This offbeat indie and DIY showcase is the place to go to find that taxidermied mouse in a tutu you've always dreamed of. There are the requisite racks of retro Levis and ironic T-shirts, but what Silver Lake Flea does well is outfit you with all the wacky home goods and tchotchkes you'll ever need.

Specializing in housewares of a more refined variety, the vendors at **Santa Monica Airport Outdoor Antique & Collectible Market** – yeah, it's a mouthful – peddle everything from Victorian and mid-century furniture to exotic plants and rare china. If you invest some time in digging through the jewelry bins, you might just find a unique bauble for a quarter of what it's worth.

The quintessential Los Angeles flea market? That's **Melrose Trading Post**. Sure, some of the "recycled" designer duds are a bit overpriced, but if you're dedicated to scouring the racks, you can end up with a statement piece in mint condition. There's also live music and an impressive assortment of food trucks. I swear, the only thing better than browsing with friends on a Sunday afternoon is stopping to enjoy a churro in the sunshine.

ROSE BOWL FLEA MARKET

Pasadena's **Rose Bowl Flea Market** is the granddaddy of all Southern California bazaars. You have to see it at least once, but the space is so huge and the options so enticing that I recommend going with a specific shopping plan (i.e. "I need a new vase and some vintage vinyl"). Otherwise, you could find yourself staggering back to your car with an empty bank account and six bags' worth of clothes, shoes, accessories, art, books and knick-knacks.

Topanga Vintage Market is a bit of a schlep out of the city proper, but once you arrive, you'll never want to leave. It's a true mélange of upscale and lowbrow. For example, I picked up my favorite pendant necklace here for a dollar, while a friend found a stunning Schiele print for $50. Plus, a trip here provides the perfect excuse to stop at picturesque Topanga State Park on the way back into the city.

MELROSE TRADING POST
7850 Melrose Avenue (at North Orange Grove Avenue; West Hollywood)
+1 323 655 7679, melrosetradingpost.org, open Sunday

ROSE BOWL FLEA MARKET
Rose Bowl Stadium, 1001 Rose Bowl Drive (near North Arroyo Boulevard;
Pasadena), +1 323 560 7469, rgcshows.com/RoseBowl.aspx
open the second Sunday of each month

SANTA MONICA AIRPORT OUTDOOR ANTIQUE & COLLECTIBLE MARKET
3050 Airport Avenue (at Cabrillo Boulevard; Santa Monica), +1 323 933 2511
santamonicaairportantiquemarket.com
open the first and fourth Sunday of each month

SILVER LAKE FLEA
1511 Micheltorena Street (near Sunset Boulevard; Silver Lake), +1 323 467 0623
silverlakeshop.com, open the second Saturday of each month

TOPANGA VINTAGE MARKET
Pierce College, Victory Boulevard at Mason Avenue (Winnetka)
+1 310 422 1844, topangavintagemarket.com
open the fourth Sunday of each month

venice

After Hollywood, Venice might just be LA's best-known neighborhood. In the 1950s and '60s, beachfront Venice established itself as a hangout for Beat poets and artists alike, and before they were inducted into rock 'n' roll history, The Doors were bohemians hanging out by the beach. These days, the neighborhood looks a little different, with rents on ultra-hip Abbot Kinney Boulevard reaching sky-high prices and companies like Snapchat opening headquarters that threaten to turn the area into "Silicon Beach". Despite all that, the area's artsy, boho spirit endures. Stroll the world-famous boardwalk, take a walk in the gorgeous, peaceful Venice Canals or enjoy the sunset from the heights of a rooftop hotel. Whatever you end up doing, Venice is bound to be a highlight of your stay.

1 Café Gratitude
2 El Huarique
3 Gjelina
4 LCD
5 Moon Juice
6 Small World Books
7 Strange Invisible Perfumes

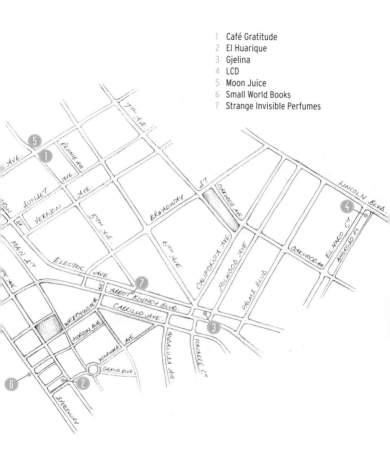

CAFÉ GRATITUDE

The definitive vegan experience

512 Rose Avenue (at 5th Avenue) / **+1 424 231 8000**
cafegratitude.com / **Open daily**

If you want to immerse yourself in the stereotypical Los Angeles healthy-living lifestyle, the first stop on your list should be Café Gratitude. The 100% organic, plant-based café has locations in Larchmont and DTLA, but the Venice Beach original is the one to visit; when you're surrounded by sun-soaked hippies, you won't feel as silly when ordering the "humble" bowl of dal, spinach and coconut mint chutney by saying, "I am humble". (Yes, they really make you order that way.) Whether you're a genuine Café Gratitude believer or you just want to get a glimpse of them in their natural habitat, the scrumptious menu is worth a visit.

EL HUARIQUE

Authentic Peruvian fare

83 Windward Avenue (near Pacific Avenue) / **+1 310 452 1254**
elhuariquevenice.com / Open daily

El Huarique started out as a tiny counter joint dishing up nosh from Peru on the Venice Boardwalk, but the beachside locale has recently found a larger home on bustling Windward Avenue. After a long day of surf, sand and sun, there's nothing like that first bite of ceviche – except for the subsequent 30 bites, that is, as the restaurant's generous portions are designed to satiate without overstuffing you. If you're not a ceviche person, try the traditional lomo saltado, a savory stir-fried mix of meat, French fries, vegetables and rice that may sound like the product of a Crockpot mishap, but tastes absolutely delicious.

GJELINA

Rustic, New American dining

**1429 Abbot Kinney Boulevard
(at Milwood Avenue)** / **+1 310 450 1429**
gjelina.com / **Open daily**

If you're chatting with a resident foodie,
there's one sentence you'll invariably hear
at some point in the conversation: "Have
you been to Gjelina yet?" Located in a
dimly lit, sexy space, Gjelina started serving
seasonal, homespun-yet-contemporary
small plates in 2008 (you must order the
buckwheat banana bread), yet the Who's
Who of the Westside food scene buzzes
about the restaurant as though it just
opened last week. The establishment's
sister bakery, Gjusta, is nearby — stop in for
a superlative latte and a house-made bialy
with lox, and sit out on the charming back
patio (or, better yet, take it to-go and have a
beach picnic on the boardwalk).

LCD

Hip, happy clothier

1919 Lincoln Boulevard (at Amoroso Place) / +1 424 500 2552
shoplcd.co / Open daily

Venice is full of trendy, minimalist boutiques, but LCD gets extra
cool-kid points for being the sole brick-and-mortar outpost of a stylish
e-commerce site. The ultra-modern online presence has translated into
a 600-square-foot boutique stocked with cult brands like Public School
and 3.1 Phillip Lim. Even if you're not in the market for upscale wares, the
sun-drenched shop is always fun to pop into when you're trawling along
swank Abbot Kinney.

MOON JUICE

The last word in fresh-pressed goodness

507 Rose Avenue (near Rennie Avenue) / **+1 310 399 2929**
moonjuiceshop.com / **Open daily**

No tour of LA's regional peculiarities is complete without a trip to Moon Juice.
Appropriately located across from Café Gratitude (see pg 102), sustainable-
juice guru Amanda Chantal Bacon's flagship location peddles several varities
of almond and coconut milks, pearl extract, and libido-enhancing, superherb-
based Sex Dust by the pound. No, Moon Juice isn't a cult, but it definitely
attracts more than its share of devotees. That said, once you try a sip of one of
the refreshing green smoothies (the Goodness Greens with celery, cucumber,
spinach, kale parsley and dandelion is delish), you might just find yourself
pledging your devotion, too.

SMALL WORLD BOOKS

Beachside bookshop

1407 Ocean Front Walk (near Horizon Avenue) / +1 310 399 2360
smallworldbooks.com / **Open daily**

Venice Beach's famous boardwalk is generally better for people-watching than shopping (unless you're in the market for a water bong or an airbrushed tee, that is), but Small World Books is the exception that proves the rule. Nestled under the bright red awning of a neighboring café, this blink-and-you'll-miss-it indie bookstore is particularly worth visiting for its carefully curated selection of Los Angeles literature, ranging from Joan Didion and John Fante to guidebooks and photography tomes. It's the perfect place to sink into a beanbag, pet the store cat and read up on local history before heading back outside to watch the sunset.

STRANGE INVISIBLE PERFUMES

Bespoke scent shop

1138 Abbot Kinney Boulevard (near San Juan Avenue)
+1 310 314 1505 / siperfumes.com / Open daily

There's no gift more Old World or elegant than custom-made perfume. That's exactly what this parfumerie offers, mixing organic botanical fragrances like Musc Botanique (geranium, frankincense, white amber and botanical musk) on site at their Venice shop. The scents are aged for a minimum of six months in a base of custom-distilled *esprit de Cognac*, the original perfumers' alcohol used in France from the 16th to 18th centuries, so, yeah, they know what they're doing. The shop sits right next to another perfume boutique, so you're pretty much guaranteed to leave the area smelling good.

LOS ANGELES AFTER DARK:
dive bars

Drown your sorrows

Don't be fooled by the glitz. At heart, Los Angeles has always been a town of starving artists, and you can still find them drinking in the city's enduring watering holes.

Nestled between boarded-up bodegas, Silver Lake's **Smog Cutter** is the dictionary definition of a dive. Come for the relaxed atmosphere, no-nonsense bartenders and dirt-cheap drinks, and stay for the late-night karaoke. Might as well since you'll be in no condition to drive after a couple of Smog Cutter's superstrong gin and tonics.

Any respectable Eastside bar crawl has to include Echo Park's **The Short Stop**. With dim lighting, a kitschy dance floor complete with a disco ball, perennially in-use pool table and a down-to-earth drink menu that won't leave you destitute, it's an easy place to be a regular, even if just for a night or two.

DTLA institution **Golden Gopher**'s understated neon sign and crowd of surly barflies are a welcome sight within this rapidly changing hood. Barroom lore has it that the Gopher, which was originally called the Golden Sun Saloon, was purchased in 1905 by President Teddy Roosevelt – I mean, how many dive bars out there can claim lofty presidential connections?

Koreatown is tops for barhopping, and any night out in K-Town has to include a visit to **HMS Bounty**. The vaguely nautical-themed pub is generous to its regular crowd, offering deals like the $5 Wiseman special (a shot of whiskey or tequila and a beer), plus, HMS Bounty sets itself apart from other bars by offering a restaurant menu that'll help sober you up in time for last call.

The Kibitz Room at Canter's is a little slice of old-school Los Angeles. Located at the back of the supremely popular all-night Canter's Deli (see pg 79), the dark cocktail lounge has doubled as a neighborhood punk rock venue since 1961. Performers from Guns N' Roses to Joni Mitchell to the Red Hot Chili Peppers have shown up for jam sessions here; even if you don't see any rock royalty, order up a sidecar (cognac, lemon juice and triple sec) and enjoy this defining LA dive.

GOLDEN GOPHER
417 West 8th Street
(near South Olive Street; Downtown), +1 213 614 8001
213dthospitality.com/goldengopher, open daily

HMS BOUNTY
3357 Wilshire Boulevard (near South Kenmore Avenue;
Koreatown), +1 213 385 7275, thehmsbounty.com
open daily

SMOG CUTTER
864 North Virgil Avenue (near Burns Avenue;
Silver Lake), +1 323 660 4626, no website, open daily

THE KIBITZ ROOM AT CANTER'S
419 North Fairfax Avenue (near Oakwood Avenue;
West Hollywood), +1 323 651 2030
cantersdeli.com/kibitz-room, open daily

THE SHORT STOP
1455 Sunset Boulevard (at Sutherland Street;
Echo Park), +1 213 482 4942, no website, open daily

THE SHORT STOP

LOS ANGELES AFTER DARK:
late-night bites

Where to find a decent meal after 2am

Pizza, nachos and other grease delivery systems have the monopoly on post-party food, but sometimes those late-night indulgences just don't hit the spot. Luckily, LA offers diverse cuisine at all hours. Whether you're heading home after a long night out, getting in to LAX in the wee hours or just an insomniac craving some real food, this city's late-late-night dinner scene will provide.

Fred 62 bills itself as being Los Feliz's neighborhood diner "for 16 years, 24 hours a day, 7 days a week," and I've been there at enough odd hours to confirm that this is the case. I've seen everyone from grandmas to studio heads to wannabe rock stars chowing down on the Juicy Lucy (a burger with cheddar that comes on brioche), fries and a milkshake in a cozy booth surrounded by the flotsam and jetsam of LA's nightlife.

Koreatown's clutch of bars, lounges and karaoke dives necessitates some killer after-midnight nosh, and **Sun Nong Dan** definitely delivers on that front. Stumble over to this traditional Korean restaurant at any hour of the day or night and feast on beef broth, ox bone soup, dumplings, braised short ribs and a whole host of other delicacies, at super-affordable prices.

If you're seeking nosh of a slightly more refined variety, **Pacific Dining Car** is the place for you. Opened in 1921 and housed in a railway train car, this Santa Monica steakhouse serves up fine-dining staples from scallops to prime rib to Maine lobster, 24/7.

101 COFFEE SHOP

Que Ricos Mexican Kitchen in North Hollywood isn't necessarily what you'd call glamorous, but the hole-in-the-wall Mexican joint on Victory Boulevard dishes out hot, appetizing plates of carne asada and tostadas 'round the clock. The menudo soup, served with house-made tortillas, always satisfies at 3am when you're longing for true sustenance.

Located in the Best Western Plus Hollywood Hills Hotel (really rolls off the tongue, doesn't it?), Franklin Village's **101 Coffee Shop** has been used as a location in tons of stuff, from *Swingers* to *Entourage*. The '60s-inspired diner cooks up comfort food like silver-dollar pancakes at all hours – which is lucky, because you haven't lived until you've tried the Cajun catfish and eggs.

101 COFFEE SHOP
6145 Franklin Avenue (at Vista Del Mar Avenue;
Hollywood), +1 323 467 1175, 101coffeeshop.com
open daily

FRED 62
1850 North Vermont Avenue (at Russell Avenue;
Los Feliz), +1 323 667 0062, fred62.com, open daily

PACIFIC DINING CAR
2700 Wilshire Boulevard (at Princeton Street;
Santa Monica), +1 310 453 4000, pacificdiningcar.com
open daily

QUE RICOS MEXICAN KITCHEN
12940 Victory Boulevard (near Coldwater Canyon
Avenue; North Hollywood), +1 818 985 8014
quericosmexicankitchen.com, open daily

SUN NONG DAN
3470 West 6th Street, #7 (near South Alexandria
Avenue; Koreatown), +1 213 365 0303, sunnongdan.com
open daily

santa monica and malibu

There's no way around it: life is just a little bit better when you're near the beach. Of course, many of us landlocked central Angelenos don't make it to the Pacific Ocean on a regular basis (sad but true – even in LA, real life tends to get in the way of sunshine), but when we do head west, it's a great reminder of why we chose to move to this crazy city in the first place. Santa Monica and Malibu have the advantages of being close to the ocean, but both neighborhoods would be worth a visit even if they were nowhere near water. For a truly unforgettable experience, get dinner in the bustling, family-friendly Santa Monica area, then drive (or book a cab) up the PCH for a drink in remote, celebrity-studded Malibu – ideally at sunset, while listening to Joni Mitchell's "Blue".

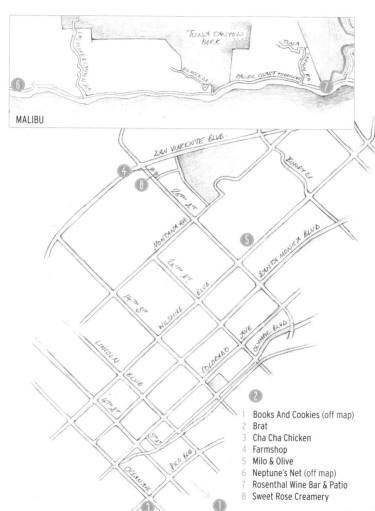

MALIBU

1 Books And Cookies (off map)
2 Brat
3 Cha Cha Chicken
4 Farmshop
5 Milo & Olive
6 Neptune's Net (off map)
7 Rosenthal Wine Bar & Patio
8 Sweet Rose Creamery

BOOKS AND COOKIES

Kid lit, treats and events

2309 Main Street (near Strand Street) / **+1 310 452 1301**
booksandcookiesla.com / **Closed Sunday**

If you bring a tyke to this Main Street bookstore and bakery, be warned; they're never, ever going to want to leave. And why would they? This multi-concept shop sells unique, gorgeous board, picture and chapter books out of a sunlit storefront that adults can appreciate, too, especially when there are daily story time sessions, arts and crafts classes and "wiggle worm fitness" activities. What's more, the staff at Books and Cookies does tons of community outreach with local organizations that serve children and families; in fact, the "cookies" part of the name is a reference to the charity cookie-decorating parties they host regularly.

BRAT

Retro clothing and punk-rock trinkets

1938 14th Street (near Pico Boulevard) / **+1 310 452 2480**
bratstore.com / **Open daily**

Looking for a compendium of David Bowie's most notable fashion moments?
How about a necklace made entirely of safety pins? You can find those and
more at Brat, an erstwhile punk rock/DIY boutique on 14th Street. It can be
tough for independent retailers to stay afloat in the area (after all, it's hard
to compete with the giant Santa Monica Promenade), but this purveyor has
attracted a cult following by treating shoppers like friends. When you swing
by, don't skip the kitchen linens and stationery adorned with four-letter
words – they are an excellent gift for a foul-mouthed friend.

CHA CHA CHICKEN

No-frills Caribbean food

1906 Ocean Avenue (at Neilson Way) / +1 310 581 1684
chachachicken.com / Open daily

Santa Monica staple Cha Cha Chicken is precisely the place to go when
you want to eat somewhere fun. The vibrant beach shack serves traditional
Caribbean fare – think jerk chicken, dirty rice and black beans, and the most
scrumptious fried plantains you've ever tasted. Unlike a lot of overpriced
oceanfront restaurants, Cha Cha Chicken doesn't harbor so much as a hint
of pretension – all food is served from the counter, and live music turns
the open-air patio into a makeshift party spot on warm summer nights.
Be advised, though: Cha Cha Chicken is BYOB, so if you really want to get
your party on, come prepared.

FARMSHOP

Artisanal bakery, restaurant and market

225 26th Street, #25 (near Georgina Avenue) / +1 310 566 2400
farmshopca.com / Open daily

Face it: you're not going to be able to escape LA without taking part in at least one artisanal farm-to-table brunch, and a fantastic place to partake in one is Farmshop. Located in the bustling, upscale Brentwood Country Mart, this is the ideal place to relax and stuff your face with the likes of avocado hummus and smoked trout omelets after a morning full of swimming, sunning and surfing. After your meal, peruse the Farmshop market's selection of curated chocolate, cheese, wine and more post-dinner treats.

MILO & OLIVE

Family-friendly gourmet cuisine

2723 Wilshire Boulevard (at Harvard Street) / **+1 310 453 6776**
miloandolive.com / **Open daily**

Early risers are rewarded at Santa Monica's beloved Milo & Olive. There are few great reasons to rise and shine, but their breakfast pizza – house-made sausage, potatoes, rosemary cream and a farm egg on a fresh-baked crust – and an Italian mimosa (made with prosecco instead of Champagne) are two of them. If you can't coax yourself out of bed in time, don't fret: the full-day menu is pretty fab, too. The wood-fired pizza is the main attraction, but the heaping plates of pasta more than hold their own, particularly the hand-rolled potato gnocchi, served with walnut basil pesto, English peas and sheep's milk feta. (Is anyone else hungry?)

NEPTUNE'S NET

Down-home seafood

42505 Pacific Coast Highway (near Yerba Buena Road)
+1 310 457 3095 / neptunesnet.com / Open daily

There's not a frill to be found at Neptune's Net, a wood-floored fish joint off the Pacific Coast Highway. This has been a Malibu landmark since 1956, and there's no better place to quench your hunger and thirst after a long day relaxing by the water. The place is delightfully gritty, with surfers and bikers alike lining the tables. My idea of heaven is a dip in the ocean at Zuma Beach, followed by one of this eatery's signature red baskets filled with fresh shrimp, Dungeness crab, a lobster roll and a cold beer. It's possible I've been known to also order the clam chowder – hey, what can I say, the ocean air makes gives me an appetite!

ROSENTHAL WINE BAR & PATIO

Carefully selected wine in a stunning beach setting

18741 Pacific Coast Highway (near Topanga Canyon Boulevard)
+1 310 456 1392 / rosenthalestatewines.com / Open daily

"You've always driven by — why not stop in?" reads one of the many road signs outside Rosenthal Wine Bar & Patio. It's pretty hard to refute that logic. The tasting room is just 10 minutes away from the Rosenthal Vineyard, and you can taste the freshness of the grapes in every glass poured. Right across from sunny Topanga State Beach, this enoteca is hard to miss thanks to the signature bright blue, larger-than-life deck chair positioned out front. When you settle on the back patio at sunset, sipping the crisp house white as live music plays in the background, you'll feel like you're on a relaxing beach vacation — somewhere a lot farther away than Malibu.

SWEET ROSE CREAMERY

Everyone's favorite ice cream

826 Pico Boulevard (near Lincoln Court) / +1 310 260 2663
sweetrosecreamery.com / Open daily

Even in a town brimming with luscious ice cream, Sweet Rose Creamery stands out. I've watched more than one child pitch a fit here, and to be honest, I understand – if someone told me I couldn't have more of the unbelievably fresh, small-batch flavors, I just might throw a tantrum, too. Such high-concept flavors as white chocolate and rose geranium have been introduced by chef Shiho Yoshikawa. Still, the classics (old-fashioned vanilla, fresh mint and their heavenly strawberry) are the creamery's true standbys; when "regular" flavors taste this good, there's no need to overthink it.

the great outdoors

Los Angeles's most beautiful hikes

BALDWIN HILLS SCENIC OVERLOOK

LA's always sunny weather is a cliché for a reason; sure, we get the occasional rainy spring and Augusts can get swampy, but most of the time, it's clear skies. Not only is this ideal for filming talkies and TV shows, but also for outdoor activities. If surfing and watersports aren't for you, you're in luck, as there is ample hiking here, allowing you to make use of the perennial 72-degree weather. (Yes, we Angelenos know you hate us.)

For a winding hike with some of the most stunning ocean views you'll find in SoCal, make the trek to **Temescal Gateway Park** in the Pacific Palisades. The area feels almost enchanted, with miles of greenery, butterflies and a waterfall. Whether you opt for the two-mile or five-mile loop, you'll get sparkling vistas either way.

Malibu was made for hiking, and the three-mile **Grotto Trail** is considered by residents to be the superlative hike in the area. The trail ends with some boulder scrambling, but then you reach a waterfall, which is perfect for cooling down after an invigorating march.

Runyon Canyon Park has attracted more than its share of celebrity Instagram posts, but the trek is good for more than star-spotting. You can tackle this relatively short loop in under two hours with your dog by your side for the classic LA experience.

The climb up to **Baldwin Hills Scenic Overlook** isn't for the faint of heart; getting up to the overlook involves a short, but strenuous set of stairs. Once you're up there, though, the panorama is spectacular – you can see the LA Basin, the San Gabriels and the Santa Monica Mountains.

Visiting the **Angeles National Forest** is like getting out of town for a full-on trip, even though it's just 30 minutes outside the city center. Climbing Strawberry Peak (so named because the mountain looks like an upside-down strawberry) is definitely a workout, but it's the stunning scenery of the mountain ranges that will leave you truly breathless.

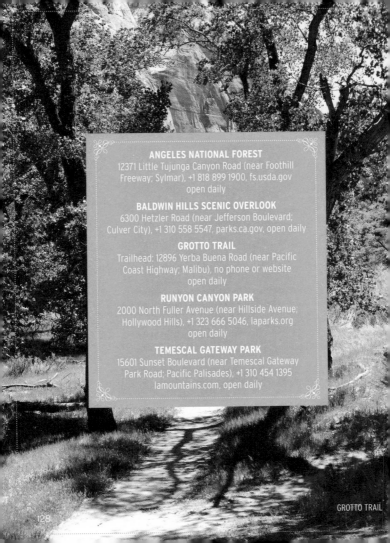

ANGELES NATIONAL FOREST
12371 Little Tujunga Canyon Road (near Foothill
Freeway; Sylmar), +1 818 899 1900, fs.usda.gov
open daily

BALDWIN HILLS SCENIC OVERLOOK
6300 Hetzler Road (near Jefferson Boulevard;
Culver City), +1 310 558 5547, parks.ca.gov, open daily

GROTTO TRAIL
Trailhead: 12896 Yerba Buena Road (near Pacific
Coast Highway; Malibu), no phone or website
open daily

RUNYON CANYON PARK
2000 North Fuller Avenue (near Hillside Avenue;
Hollywood Hills), +1 323 666 5046, laparks.org
open daily

TEMESCAL GATEWAY PARK
15601 Sunset Boulevard (near Temescal Gateway
Park Road; Pacific Palisades), +1 310 454 1395
lamountains.com, open daily

GROTTO TRAIL